book *of* faith
Advent Reflections
I Wonder as I Wander

book *of* faith
Advent Reflections
I Wonder as I Wander

Ted Schroeder
Kari Reiquam
Andrew D. Hagen
Kay S. Richter
Debbie Trafton O'Neal

Book of Faith is an initiative of the
Evangelical Lutheran Church in America
God's work. Our hands.

Contents

Introduction

Advent traditions have been around for a long time. One tradition still observed in many congregations and homes is lighting a candle for each of the four weeks in the Advent season. In many places, the candles are named Hope (the first week), Love (the second week), Joy (the third week), and Peace (the fourth week).

Hope, love, joy, and *peace* also show up at this time of year in Christmas greetings we send or receive, in banners and decorations in our churches and homes, and even in songs that we hear or sing. But do these four words still mean something for us and for the world today?

Advent Reflections invites you to spend some time wondering about hope, love, joy, and peace. Is hope still alive? Does love always find a way? What gives joy to the world? Will nations—and next-door neighbors—ever be at peace? These are just a few of the questions that might make us wonder. This book also encourages you to wonder at the hope, love, joy, and peace that God gives through Jesus—the reason for our hope. The baby in a manger shows God's way of love in the world. He is our joy-bringer and Prince of Peace. Take time during this busy season to stop and wonder at who God is and what God has done. What do you wonder as you wander on your journey of faith, through the pages of the Bible, toward Christmas?

Advent Reflections continues a centuries-old tradition of using the time before Christmas to reflect on and prepare for the celebration of Jesus' birth. The benefits of this practice come largely from spending time each day in Bible reading, reflection, and discussion. You can connect this with things you already do in your daily routine. Read the Bible text, reflection, and prayer during a meal, coffee break, or bus ride. Consider the "Questions to Ponder" as you take a walk or spend some quiet time thinking and praying. When you are with friends and family members, talk about what you are reading and learning. Use the activities in this book for hands-on Advent experiences. Discuss the Bible study questions in a group that already exists, or form a group with other people who are reading this book.

Advent Reflections is a Book of Faith resource. In 2007 the Evangelical Lutheran Church in America (ELCA) affirmed the centrality of the Bible to Christian life and faith, and at the same time recognized the reality of biblical illiteracy in the church. This resulted in the Book of Faith initiative, which invites us to open Scripture and join the conversation. By looking at the Bible through different lenses—historical, literary, Lutheran, and devotional—we can enter into a dialogue with God's Word in ways that lead to deeper understanding and spiritual growth. The emphasis in this book is on the devotional lens, but the other lenses are used to provide insights into Scripture as well. As a Book of Faith resource, *Advent Reflections* offers opportunities to open Scripture, look at it through different lenses, and join conversations with the Bible, with friends or family, with a small group, and ultimately, with God.

How to Use This Book

Start this book on the first Sunday in Advent (four Sundays before Christmas), if possible. Put it in a prominent place in your home, purse, backpack, or briefcase, so you'll be reminded to read it every day.

Advent Reflections

In this section, you'll find two pages of reflection, questions, and a prayer for every day in Advent. Have a Bible handy so you can read the text, then read the reflection. The "Questions to Ponder" provide ways for you to spend some time thinking about what you've read. Close your devotional time with the prayer, perhaps followed by a prayer of your own or a few moments of silence. Open your heart to the Spirit's work during this season of wonder.

Bible Studies

This book provides a Bible study for each week in Advent. Use the Bible study pages on your own, with a friend or family member, or in a group. If you are in a small group using the Bible studies in this book, take time for the daily Advent reflections as well.

Activities

The Activities section describes many ways for families with younger children to celebrate the wonder of Advent. You might want to look through this entire section before Advent begins and pick out one or two activities for each week, or simply choose activities as the season goes along. Either way, focus on what is most doable and meaningful for your family, not on finishing every activity that is provided.

Please note that the Wonderful Luminaries activity builds each week in Advent. During Week 1 you create a Hope luminary to light and set out. During the next weeks, you add a Love luminary, then a Joy luminary, and finally a Peace luminary. Made of durable materials, your set of Wonderful Luminaries could easily be stored and brought out each Advent for many years to come.

Our Writers

Week 1 Reflections and Bible Study: I Wonder about Hope

Ted Schroeder served as a parish pastor in Illinois, Ohio, and Minnesota for 15 years, and then as director for resource development and director for education for the Division for Congregational Ministries, ELCA, for 16 years. He is the author of many books, studies, congregational resources, and articles for magazines including *AAL Correspondent* and *Thrivent.* Now retired, Ted lives in Plymouth, Minnesota, cherishing wife, Ellen, three children, and five grandchildren.

Week 2 Reflections and Bible Study: I Wonder about Love

Kari Reiquam lives in the mountains of Colorado and serves First Lutheran Church in Gypsum. Ordained in 1979, she followed paths of ministry in Arizona, New Mexico, Oregon, and Hawaii. Her husband, Bryan Austill, and daughters, Siri and Annelise, travel the hills and valleys of life with her.

Week 3 Reflections and Bible Study: I Wonder about Joy

Andrew D. Hagen is on the pastoral team at Advent Lutheran Church in Boca Raton, Florida. He has coauthored two books available from Augsburg Fortress, *Joyful Harvest* and *A Story Worth Sharing*, and written devotions for *Christ in Our Home* and *The Word in Season*. He is also a contributor to *The Clergy Journal*, a monthly columnist for *Boca Life Magazine*, and a coach and consultant in the area of congregational strategic planning. In the fall of 2010, Andy will bike through the state of Florida to raise awareness and funds for the Lazarus Project, which plans to open a new health center in Haiti.

Week 4 Reflections and Bible Study: I Wonder about Peace

Kay S. Richter received a master of divinity degree from Luther Seminary in 1991 and a bachelor of arts degree in English and Classical Studies from Michigan State University in 1987. She has also studied New Testament in the doctoral program at Vanderbilt University. Kay has served congregations in Minnesota, South Dakota, and Wisconsin, where she currently serves. She also enjoys teaching for Synod Lay School programs, especially courses in New Testament, Old Testament, and Biblical Greek.

Activities

Debbie Trafton O'Neal is an author, educator, and consultant who lives in the Seattle, Washington, area. She has written more than 50 books for children, families, and educators, and has developed, written, and edited curriculum for more than 25 years. Creative, hands-on experiences are her favorite ways to teach and learn!

Advent Reflections

Week 1: I Wonder about Hope

Day 1: Sunday

High Hopes

2 Corinthians 3:4-18

> 🔲 *Key Verse:* Since, then, we have such a hope, we act with great
> boldness. 2 Corinthians 3:12

The thumping sound woke us. "What is that?" I said. "It sounds like something falling outside the window," my wife replied. We began an early morning search. The noise turned out to be a determined robin in the pine tree in the front yard. He was watching his reflection in the bedroom window. He apparently decided that the reflection was a rival, so he kept flying at the image in an effort to drive it away. Amazingly persistent, he flew against the window again and again. He reminded me of the ram in the song "High Hopes." According to the song, the ram kept butting a dam, hoping to do it in, because he had "high hopes, high apple pie in the sky hopes." Certainly that robin did, too.

Of course, hoping to accomplish the impossible is easy for a robin and a ram. They don't think things through, calculate the likelihood of success, look to outcomes. We are certainly smarter than that. When we are faced with an impossible situation, we calculate the possibility of success. We tend to rely on our own strengths and abilities. As a result, we often back off, save ourselves, hide, turn away. Great hurts and fears can overwhelm us. Who can face, "You have perhaps two months to live"? Who can deal with, "Your son has been in an accident," or "The money is all gone"? Those situations go beyond our own strength. Then we need a powerful hope. The apostle Paul says, "Since, then, we have such a hope [that is, a hope in Jesus Christ], we act with great boldness" (2 Corinthians 3:12).

The grace of God, given to us in Jesus, emboldens us. We are not in the clutches of a random fate. We rest in the power and enjoy the presence of God.

Sometimes when things go wrong or something threatens, people say, "Oh, if only this would go away or we could find a way." That is more of a wish than a hope.

Our hope is not a wispy wish that things will turn out all right sometime in the future. Our hope is bold, strong, and grounded in the death and resurrection of Jesus. That ultimate hope helps us transcend all the barriers we face. We have, says Paul, "great boldness." Jesus said, "For God all things are possible" (Matthew 19:26).

Without hope, our lives turn to ashes. "Hope sees the invisible, feels the intangible, and achieves the impossible" (author unknown). We are sent and equipped to accomplish the impossible by the grace of God and the power of the Spirit.

Questions to Ponder

- When have you faced an impossible situation? What did your hope in Jesus Christ have to do with overcoming that obstacle?
- For you, what is the difference between a wish and a hope?

Prayer

Lord, turn us from our need to depend on our own strength to deal with the impossibles in life. Embolden us by your Spirit, so that we may enjoy the wonder of a hope made sure in Jesus. Help us to share that hope with others. In Jesus' name. Amen.

Day 2: Monday

Taking On the Giants

1 Samuel 17:1-50; Romans 15:1-6

Key Verse: For whatever was written in former days was written for our instruction, so that by steadfastness and by the encouragement of the scriptures we might have hope. Romans 15:4

In the inspiring story of David and Goliath (see 1 Samuel 17:1-50), the little guy wins. He beats the giant. How about us?

I took on a giant. The giant's name was cancer, and it came to stay with me.

The surgery was supposed to have been routine. Afterward, the doctor came in muttering something about "quite a malignancy." At that moment, the giant came and sat down next to me. And my life changed.

At any waking moment, I watched the giant. It seemed to turn my future in its fingers and pick at every thread of joy or hope, every dream, everything I cherished. And there was nothing I could do or say, nothing I could invent or imagine to take all of that back again.

In my dark dreams I shouted at the giant, "Get away from me! Go sit with someone else. Breathe your deadly breath on some other person more deserving of your visit. How can you be here? Who let you in here? Who sent you? Did God send you? Did God send you to bring me down?"

And even in my dreams, the giant sat silently and smiled at me.

The pit of my pain and self-pity grew deeper and darker. I could no longer climb the sides of the pit and see the future. The shackles of my own fear and anger froze me. Buried in that pit, I wept for myself and for my dreams and for what might have been.

And still the giant sat silently and smiled at me.

But there in the deepest place in the pit—there, somehow from the echoes of my memory, these words came to me: "For I am convinced that neither death, nor life, nor angels, nor rulers, nor things present, nor things to come, nor powers, nor height, nor depth, nor anything else in all creation, will be able to separate us from the love of God in Christ Jesus our Lord" (Romans 8:38-39).

And I had hope again.

I live outside the pit now, but not far outside. I'm always on the edge, wondering and waiting. But there's a difference. Now God has placed the cross of Jesus Christ between me and the giant.

And in that promise of the cross, from the edge of the pit of my own despair, I stare back at the giant and smile.

Questions to Ponder

- When have you been visited by a giant? What was the giant's name?
- How do God's Word and the Spirit's power give you hope in the face of giants?

Prayer

Lord, give us not only courage to face the future, but the strength and faith to stand firmly in your promises and to live in and share real hope. Amen.

Day 3: Tuesday

People of Hope

Romans 12:1-12

🔖 *Key Verse:* Rejoice in hope. Romans 12:12

I've known a few people who live in hope. Perhaps you have too, but not very many. They seem hard to come by these days.

People of hope don't necessarily have the Spirit in their hands. Busyness—even busyness at very good things—does not always mark a hope-filled person.

People of hope don't necessarily have the Spirit in their feet. Trotting fretfully along one's spiritual journey doesn't make one particularly hopeful.

People of hope don't always have the Spirit in their heads. Lofty theological thoughts sometimes seem to go round and round in the same cranial circles. And they do not necessarily create hope.

People of hope have the Spirit in their eyes. They see life differently. It's pretty easy, as the years go by, to get turned around and gaze longingly at the past. It's pretty easy these days to count the signs of death and decay in ourselves, in society, in the culture, in the system, in the direction we all are going. It is easy to become prophets of rightly projected gloom—or doom. And prophet-like people who call others to account, those who call others to repentance, are certainly needed. But they are not always people of hope.

People of hope have life in their eyes. They approach today as though it leans into tomorrow. They see today as though it is lighted by the gift of tomorrow. They have a sense of eternity about them. They look up. They call others to look up with them. Because they lean into God's future, they give today away. Because they lean into tomorrow, they project hope. Because they lean into tomorrow, they live in peace and joy.

Questions to Ponder

- Name someone you know who shines with hope. Describe what that person means to you.
- When is hope most important for you? Where does it come from and where does it lead you?

Prayer

Lord, we are called to many tasks. Give us not only the energy and will to accomplish our tasks, but also eyes of hope that lead us to move with anticipation and look for miraculous outcomes. Amen.

Day 4: Wednesday

In the Midst of Life

1 Thessalonians 4:13-18

> *Key Verse:* But we do not want you to be uninformed, brothers and sisters, about those who have died, so that you may not grieve as others do who have no hope. 1 Thessalonians 4:13

We gathered solemnly around the grave, as was the custom. The family, all dressed in dark tones, sat at the front of the gathering, as was the custom. Many shed tears, as was the custom. As pastor, I stood at the head of the casket and read the opening of the graveside service, as was the custom. Almost without thinking, I intoned the customary words: "In the midst of life, we are in death." Everything that day was customary and expected, except the weather. Instead of being dark and rainy, as one might expect, this funeral was held on one of those remarkable May days when the very air sparkles with sunlight and the earth seems to breathe new life.

Just off to the side, a little beyond the edge of the gathering of mourners, the day just became too much for some children who had come along with their families. They began to play. Soon they were running and giggling (as children do) among the gravestones and around some of the trees. Their laughter got louder as they forgot where they were and celebrated the beautiful day.

I began to speak louder. The children did not notice, but everyone noticed the children. Some of the parents began to scurry around trying to corral the boisterous gang. Nothing seemed to work. Of course, the sounds were contagious. More and more of the mourners found themselves trying to hide a broadening smile. And I found myself saying the Lord's Prayer and benediction through a half-hidden grin, backed by the playground sounds of a gaggle of gleeful children who would not be silenced.

"I do not know why parents cannot keep their children under control," the funeral director fumed as soon as he could get to me after the service. "You'd think they would know better."

As people began to leave, I shared the expected condolences with the family. And then I went over and thanked the children for being there.

It occurred to me that we probably should have a few playing and laughing children at every graveside service—not just to break the gloom—but to remind us of our hope. If it is true that "in the midst of life we are in death," for us, as followers of the Risen One, it is truer that "in the midst of death, we are in life."

Questions to Ponder

- How is the funeral of a believer different from that of someone else? What does it mean to grieve "differently"?
- "How can you people be so happy at a sad time like this?" If someone asked you that at a funeral, what would you say?

Prayer

Lord, we seek your presence and comfort in those times of sadness that we cannot avoid. Help us not to despair, and strengthen our trust in the hope that we are given in the risen Jesus. Amen.

Day 5: Thursday

A Hope-Filled Heart

1 Peter 5:6-11

Key Verse: Cast all your anxiety on him, because he cares for you.
1 Peter 5:7

By most standards, she had a lot to complain about. She had lived long enough to "show her age," as she said it. Her husband had died many years before, and she had lived long enough to see several of her children die, too. She lived in a very run-down house at the edge of town. Her health was failing. Her heart troubled her; her eyesight failed. She didn't get out much.

And yet Dorothy was rarely alone. People often stopped to see her. Children came to "play," they said. Wherever she went, Dorothy was the center of attention. And all because she could laugh. No one could laugh like Dorothy. Laughter exploded from her at almost any excuse. And she shook herself and the rafters with her laughter. Invariably Dorothy would begin to laugh, and then the children would catch the laughter and join her. And then the adults would join in, and finally all would be enveloped in gales of laugher. Dorothy was the ingredient needed at most church gatherings, where everyone took themselves and their issues much too seriously.

"How do you do it, Dorothy?" I asked her. "How do you live such an upbeat life and find it in yourself to laugh all the time?"

She smiled and laughed a little. "Easy," she said. "I live a life of hope by choice. I have a choice each morning. I can keep the day for myself and worry my way into feeling really down and discouraged. Or I can look at the day as a gift. I can look up and give the day with its troubles and worries away. I choose to give it away. Since it is not my day, I don't have to solve all the world's problems or make things better. I just look forward with hope for what I know God has in store for me and celebrate. 'Thank you, God,' I say. And laugh."

Questions to Ponder

- What does it mean to you to "give the day away"? What happens when you are able to do that?
- What difference would it make in your life and relationships if you lived a hope-filled life?

Prayer

Lord, so many things fill our hearts. Some things we cherish and some we dread. Open our hearts to your loving presence, and fill us with hope and joy as we face the future. In Jesus' name. Amen.

Day 6: Friday

We Still Have Jesus

Romans 5:1-11

> *Key Verse:* We also boast in our sufferings, knowing that suffering produces endurance, and endurance produces character, and character produces hope, and hope does not disappoint us. Romans 5:3-5

For Mom and Dad and the children, the song was one of their favorites. They listened to it often. They all knew the song so well that they sang it even when it wasn't playing:

In the morning, when I rise
In the morning, when I rise
In the morning, when I rise
Give me Jesus.

Give me Jesus,
Give me Jesus.
You can have all this world,
Just give me Jesus.
   —African American spiritual

Then it happened. The storm. Worse than many before. It tore through the town and took several houses, including theirs. Afterward they stood in the yard. "All gone! It's all gone!" Dad said. The children were weeping. Mom tried to pick up things they were unable to save before they ran into the cellar. "All gone!" Dad said again. Seven-year-old Samantha looked over the devastation as she heard her family crying. "But we still have Jesus, don't we? Don't we still have Jesus?" she said.

After the rebuilding of the house and the remaking of their lives, the family kept and treasured Samantha's phrase. Often, when things went wrong, when someone was down and troubled, someone else would say, "But we still have Jesus, don't we? We still have Jesus."

No one likes troubles or trials. No one looks forward to pain or suffering. Troubles and sufferings drive us down, to be sure. They can turn us in on ourselves and make us draw away from others. They can send us into times of self-pity and private weeping. But even the dark times drive us back to the Savior who promised to be with us always "to the ends of the earth." As followers of the Risen One, we can look at even troubles or suffering with hope.

"Suffering produces endurance, and endurance produces character, and character produces hope, and hope does not disappoint us," Paul says. Whatever the trouble, pain, or trial, with confidence we can say, "We still have Jesus."

Questions to Ponder

- What do you turn to in times of trouble or suffering? How does this help you and others?
- How is the hope that suffering produces different from wishing for a better future?

Prayer

Lord, be with us with your powerful promise. We depend on your presence to bring us through times of trouble or pain. Make the hope made possible by your death and resurrection shine in our future. Remind us that whatever happens, we still have Jesus. In his name. Amen.

Day 7: Saturday

Gone to the Cross

John 12:12-15

> *Key Verse:* So they took branches of palm trees and went out to meet him, shouting, "Hosanna! Blessed is the one who comes in the name of the Lord—the King of Israel!" John 12:13

The people celebrated as this man rode into Jerusalem. They knew that his coming was a claim to be the king, the deliverer. "Hosanna!" ("The Lord saves" or "Save us, Lord"), they shouted. They had hope because of the promise carried by this rider king. They welcomed him. They threw branches and clothes before him. They shouted their hope that he would bring them freedom from oppression and the many blessings that God had promised.

A few days later the people were shouting something else: "Crucify him!" What happened? Their hopes were dashed. Jesus certainly didn't seem to be a king now. He was an arrested and condemned usurper—a fraud. The hopes of the people marched with him to the cross and seemed to die there.

This feeling is not new to us. Many of our hopes and dreams seem to crumble and turn to dust right before our eyes. "You can't have that," or "You can't do that," or "You aren't entitled to that," we hear too often. With the people of Jerusalem, we see our hopes go to the cross.

And yet the hopes of the hosanna shouters did not die on the cross. Those hopes were raised and perfected on Sunday in the resurrection of Jesus. Once again the people were able to cry after the risen Savior, "Blessed is the one who comes in the name of the Lord. Hosanna!"

Where can we go with our shattered hopes and broken dreams? When our hopes seem to go to the cross and die, what can we do besides mourn what might have been? With the people of Jerusalem and the disciples, we follow Jesus to the tomb. There at the empty tomb our hopes are renewed, as we receive not simply things we hoped for, but far more—forgiveness and life in him.

"Hosanna!" we still can shout. This word is not only for the time of Lent as we journey to the cross and prepare for Easter. It is also for now, in the time of

Advent, when we await the coming of the Christ child. "Hosanna," we say as we celebrate Emmanuel, God with us. In the child who is born, we are taken to the cross and to the empty tomb so that we can continue to shout, "Hosanna!"

Questions to Ponder

- What might you have felt or experienced if you were in the crowd that welcomed Jesus into Jerusalem and in the crowd that called for his crucifixion?
- What hopes do you have because of Jesus?

Prayer

Lord, renew our hopes and keep us always looking forward to the gifts we receive in the death and resurrection of Jesus. Help us welcome him with praise and celebrate him as our Savior. In his name. Amen.

Week 2: I Wonder about Love

Day 8: Sunday

Love's Ups and Downs

Luke 1:46-55

💬 *Key Verse:* He has brought down the powerful from their thrones, and lifted up the lowly; he has filled the hungry with good things, and sent the rich away empty. Luke 1:52-53

In *Our Lady of the Lost and Found: A Novel of Mary, Faith, and Friendship* (Penguin, 2002), writer Diane Schoemperlen imagines a Monday in which an ordinary woman walks into her living room to discover Mary, the mother of God, standing next to a houseplant. Mary is wearing a trench coat (blue, of course) and white Nikes, and has a shawl over her head. She has come because she is in need of some rest, and asks if she might stay for a while. The ordinary woman invites Mary to stay for as long as she needs, and her life no longer seems ordinary by the time Mary leaves.

Mary the servant girl travels under the radar of our attention, relating to those who have lost their way, those who have no home and no name, unseen and unheard. She challenges and surprises us. She brings a song as her gift. In her song, we hear of the little ones of this world, fragile people whose struggle is on the surface for all to see. We hear that God is different than we might think. Rather than favoring the rich and the powerful, God has favored Mary. She is part of a pattern of God's loving encounter with the world—a pattern in which the lowly are lifted high and the high are brought low, the hungry are filled and the filled are emptied.

Mary shakes up our assumptions about what is important and what to strive for. She helps us to look at things that may have seemed insignificant to us before. She helps to prepare us to see Jesus and what he does as part of God's loving pattern. And in doing that, she points to a path of life that leads to God and leads to love.

This week, let's invite Mary to our homes, to our ordinary lives, to our everyday work. Let's invite her to sing to us as we wander and to accompany us as we wonder about God's way of love. Let Mary rest with us, imagine with us, and challenge us to see our ordinary lives in a new way.

Questions to Ponder

- If Mary came to visit you this week, what could she bring that you need? What would you like to share with her?
- What is it about Mary's song that provokes you? What is it that makes you wonder about God and the way that God loves?

Prayer

O loving God of the highs and lows, Mary's song challenges us and inspires our imaginations. Bring your Spirit of love into our lives, that we may imagine ourselves in your loving gaze and imagine a world in which both the lofty and the lowly discover the meaning of your love. Amen.

Day 9: Monday

Released for Love

Luke 3:1-17

> *Key Verse:* Prepare the way of the Lord, make his paths straight. Every valley shall be filled, and every mountain and hill shall be made low, and the crooked shall be made straight, and the rough ways made smooth; and all flesh shall see the salvation of God. Luke 3:4-6

The arrival of the Lord moves and shakes the world. The geography changes— the hills are lowered and the valleys are raised up!

The arrival of the Lord moves and shakes people, too. God is intent on all people seeing God's loving work of salvation. Imagine people on the hills and people in the valleys—if the hills came down and the valleys came up, everyone would be on level ground, seeing eye-to-eye. This sounds a lot like Mary's song (Luke 1:46-55), the reversal of "the way things are." Some are brought down and some are lifted up.

John the Baptist was a mover and shaker who prepared the way of the Lord, God's way of love. John's proclamation of a baptism for forgiveness of sin was a challenge to the religious authorities of the time and a release for people who needed to be raised up to serve in the name of love. No longer did people have to "pay their dues" to gain God's favor with fees and sacrifices given in the temple. People could begin again and connect with God in the waters of baptism in the Jordan River. Forgiveness of sins released people to a life-involving and life-giving relationship with God.

John also challenged the Roman authorities who ruled the land at the time. He challenged those who served the Roman Empire to use their power to serve and not exploit the people. He called people to live in abundance and share with others in response to God, rather than live in the poverty of indebtedness to Rome. He called people to see that they did not belong to Rome—they belonged to God, who called them to serve freely in the name of love.

John's life and message of preparing the way of the Lord continue to move and shake people today. John challenges those who have power and comforts those who are oppressed. He calls all people to be baptized, receive forgiveness, and enjoy a relationship with God. He challenges us to see God's direction and God's way of love and to live lives that make a difference to others. He calls us to serve freely in the name of love, as part of God's love at work in the world.

Questions to Ponder

- What would a new start mean for you?
- Where do you see God's love at work in the world? How are you a part of this?

Prayer

O God, give us a new start. Make your way in our lives and in the world. Lead us down from our mountaintop perches and up from our burdened valleys to walk in love and follow your call. Amen.

Day 10: Tuesday

Love Widens the Circle

Luke 4:16-30

> *Key Verse:* He unrolled the scroll and found the place where it was written: "The Spirit of the Lord is upon me, because he has anointed me to bring good news to the poor. He has sent me to proclaim release to the captives and recovery of sight to the blind, to let the oppressed go free, to proclaim the year of the Lord's favor."
> Luke 4:17-19

In 1981 a young mother in Tanzania was carried to a hospital. She had contracted gangrene in one leg. It was not only spreading, but becoming life threatening. The doctors decided that the woman's leg needed to be amputated to save her life. They explained this to the woman, but she refused to have the surgery. For several days they tried to convince her, and she continued to refuse.

Then the doctors found out why the woman was refusing a lifesaving procedure. According to her tribe's customs and beliefs, if someone had a limb cut off, the tribe would cut him or her out. She would not be allowed back into this tribe if her leg were amputated.

The doctors decided to see if the tribe would reconsider this custom, so they called the elders of the tribe together. For several days the elders sat on the hospital grounds, debating and debating. Finally, they came up with a decision. The woman could come back after losing her leg, but she would have to live on the edges of the circle of the village. She would be on the margins—not really part of the tribe, yet not completely thrown out. She would be treated as a "nobody" who would not be eligible to receive tribal justice or humanitarian treatment.

While the elders deliberated, the woman began to worship with the church community that had been established near the hospital. She learned about baptism and a new community of people of all tribes and races.

When the woman heard the verdict that she would live on the margins of the village, she refused to go back to her tribe. She decided to have the surgery and live in a new "tribe" that would welcome her into the community, broken as she was. Soon after the surgery, she was baptized in the church and began a new life on the hospital grounds.

Questions to Ponder

- Who are those inside the circle of your community or congregation? Who are those on the margins of your community or congregation?
- What would happen if the circle grew wider? What is preventing this from happening?

Prayer

O God, thank you for including us in the circle of your love. Your arms have a wide embrace! Widen the circle of our embrace and hospitality, in Jesus' name and by Jesus' claim. Amen.

Day 11: Wednesday

Love Bends and Lifts

Luke 13:10-17

> 💬 *Key Verse:* She was bent over and was quite unable to stand up straight. When Jesus saw her, he called her over and said, "Woman, you are set free from your ailment." Luke 13:11-12

It was 10:30 on a January night in the Denver International Airport. The couple's flight had been canceled. For an hour they tried to arrange a new flight, but the winds were too high. There would be no way to leave that evening.

They went downstairs to retrieve their luggage at the baggage claim office—a dreary place on a cold January night with planeloads of abandoned and frustrated people lined up to get their bags. The light was dim from fluorescent bulbs, and the air was filled with the weary anger and bitter disappointment of people left to face a night in the airport or an unwanted hotel.

Stranded passengers lined up in front of three women at computers, their faces lit by the screens. Passengers took turns reciting their names and flight numbers, while the women at the computers typed away. Sometimes there was an outburst when the news was bad and a bag was not found. Then the woman at the screen, accused, would bend lower, trying to be invisible.

After about 30 minutes, the couple moved to the front of the line. The woman at the screen did not look up. Hunched over the keyboard, she met the couple with these words: "There probably is not much I can do. There is only one person left on duty in baggage, so there is no guarantee you'll get your bags tonight."

She acted cornered.

Then the man said, "We know this isn't your doing. We would like to say, first, that we appreciate that you are here on a night like this, doing a job that is difficult to do. Thank you for being of service to us and to all the people in this room."

The woman looked up and then looked him in the eye. Light from the computer screen revealed her smile. "That is the first 'thank you' I've gotten today. Thank *you*, sir."

The couple left the room, lifted. Yes, their bags were found, but more than that, they saw what a gracious word of release can do.

Questions to Ponder

- Think about a time when you were "bent over" and someone lifted you to new vision and purpose. How did that feel?
- How can you share God's love and compassion with "bent-over" people in your world?

Prayer

O God, you see us with eyes of love. When we are bent over with illness, pain, worry, or sadness, you touch us and lift us to praise. Give us grace to reach out to others, that all may be lifted to praise you and share your compassion. Amen.

Day 12: Thursday

Rich with Love

Luke 18:18-27

> 🗨 *Key Verse:* When Jesus heard this, he said to him, "There is still one thing lacking. Sell all that you own and distribute the money to the poor, and you will have treasure in heaven; then come, follow me." But when he heard this, he became sad; for he was very rich.
> Luke 18:22-23

The man talking to Jesus was very rich. Not only did he have great wealth; his life was filled up, stuffed, with no room for anything else. He was doing all that was expected and had no room in his life for mercy, compassion, and kindness. When Jesus invited him to make room for the poor, to make room for love in a new way, the man was sad.

In the book *Passages in Caregiving: Turning Chaos into Confidence* (William Morrow, 2010), Gail Sheehy describes men and women who make room in their lives to care for an elderly parent or a chronically ill spouse. She tells of a veteran actor who had just started a job on a popular TV series when his mother was diagnosed with Alzheimer's disease. He first arranged for home health aides and then moved her into an assisted living facility, but he found the care lacking. He realized that she needed him in her life, and he found a way to restructure his life around her. He met her for lunch and took her to movies, curtailing his social life and travel. Once a year he and his mother walked in an annual fundraiser for the Alzheimer's Association. They made their journey public and became part of the Alzheimer's community.

For six years the man cared for his mother. There were exhausting times. However, two years after she died, he said, "I miss it, even the hard stuff; it's all valuable."

Jesus invites us, like the rich ruler, to enjoy a fuller, more meaningful life than money or wealth can bring—a life rich with sharing God's love with others. He invites us to make room in our lives for love, and to share the treasures of his mercy.

Questions to Ponder

- What fills your life? What makes your life rich?
- What would need to happen to make room in your life for sharing God's love with others?

Prayer

Living God, you invite us to a richer, fuller life than we could ever imagine. Make room in our lives for love and fill us with the treasures of your mercy, so that we can share your love and mercy with others. Amen.

Day 13: Friday

Extravagant Love

Luke 7:36-50

> *Key Verse:* And a woman in the city, who was a sinner, having learned that [Jesus] was eating in the Pharisee's house, brought an alabaster jar of ointment. She stood behind him at his feet, weeping, and began to bathe his feet with her tears and to dry them with her hair. Then she continued kissing his feet and anointing them with the ointment. . . . "Therefore, I tell you, her sins, which were many, have been forgiven; hence she has shown great love. But the one to whom little is forgiven, loves little." Luke 7:37-38, 47

A banquet of thanksgiving was held to celebrate the 25th anniversary of the ordination of Lutheran women. All were seated at tables, ready for the usual banquet fare, when they were surprised by a trumpet fanfare. People looked up to see a row of waiters in tuxedos, ceremoniously marching into the room. Large platters of roasted turkeys were lifted high over the waiters' heads. When the waiters reached the front of the room, they stopped to bow and the audience cheered. Then they grandly moved throughout the room, placing a turkey on each table. Someone at each table was given an apron and a knife, and the turkeys were carved and served for all to see. The meal was a lavish gesture of celebration and grace and joy.

In the Gospel of Luke, Jesus declares his mission early on (4:18-19) and repeats it in Luke 7:22: "Go and tell John what you have seen and heard: the blind receive their sight, the lame walk, the lepers are cleansed, the deaf hear, the dead are raised, the poor have good news brought to them." Later in the same chapter, Jesus is eating at someone's house when a woman comes, uninvited, surprising the host and guests. This "sinner" comes with an alabaster jar of ointment and makes a lavish gesture of covering Jesus' feet with tears and ointment. She is overcome with joy because Jesus has released her from sin. Her lavish gesture of love is her response to the good news that God has recognized, welcomed, and claimed her in an extravagant love.

During the Advent season, we prepare for the coming of Jesus. The baby born in a manger is a lavish gift of love from God to us. God holds nothing back here. This is God's Son, after all, who lives, suffers, dies, and is raised to life again. Through him, we receive forgiveness, grace, and new life. What extravagant love!

Questions to Ponder

- How do you feel about the extravagance of God's love?
- How can you celebrate God's extravagant love?

Prayer

O God, you surprise us with your abundance and pour out your love in extravagant ways. Set us free from all that holds us back from celebrating and sharing your love and grace. Amen.

Day 14: Saturday

Love Changes Things

Luke 19:1-10

Key Verse: Zacchaeus stood there and said to the Lord, "Look, half of my possessions, Lord, I will give to the poor; and if I have defrauded anyone of anything, I will pay back four times as much." Then Jesus said to him, "Today salvation has come to this house." Luke 19:8-9

Zacchaeus was a tax collector who exploited others and hoarded everything he owned. When Jesus comes along, Zacchaeus goes up in a tree to see him. He comes down from the tree when Jesus invites himself to Zacchaeus's home.

When Jesus comes to his house, Zacchaeus is connected to God and to others, and he changes his ways. His life is turned around by Jesus' visit. He practices charity *and* justice. Instead of hanging on to what he has, he gives half of it away. Instead of exploiting others, he no longer takes more tax than what is due and amply repays people he has cheated. The gifts of God's love and salvation enable Zacchaeus to empty himself for others.

In the book *The Blue Sweater: Bridging the Gap between Rich and Poor in an Interconnected World* (Rodale Books, 2010), Jacqueline Novogratz tells of going to Africa as a banker. One day she is jogging down a dusty street when she sees a young boy wearing a blue sweater. He is so skinny that the sweater comes to his knees. She stops and runs to the boy because she recognizes the sweater. She had given away the sweater long ago. She checks the tag on the back and her name is still there! The sweater had made its way from Alexandria, Virginia, her childhood home, to Kigali, the capital of Rwanda, where she was starting her career.

This remarkable coincidence connects her with the boy and with the people of Africa. She now sees herself in a different relationship with the people she serves. She begins to change the way she relates to them financially. She tries to share money in ways that empower the receiver to be responsible. Her journey is not over. She has not found the answer to life's inequalities and challenges, but she continues to explore ways that all people can live in mutual interdependence and respect.

Questions to Ponder

- If Jesus came to your house, how would that change things?
- How does God's love affect the way you deal with people in your family, your community, and the world?

Prayer

O God, your love widens our circle and changes things so that we can no longer think only about ourselves. Fill us and strengthen us with your grace. Help us to share your love and blessings with people in need around the world. Amen.

Week 3: I Wonder about Joy

Day 15: Sunday

Neither Rain nor Snow

Luke 2:8-15

> *Key Verse:* But the angel said to them, "Do not be afraid; for see—I am bringing you good news of great joy for all the people." Luke 2:10

Our neighbors do not appear to be eager to receive any news, good or otherwise. An errant vehicle hit their mailbox post a few weeks ago and snapped it neatly in half. Leaning sadly next to its former support is the aggrieved mailbox. I have begun to wonder when some more functional repair might be undertaken. I picture the postal carrier driving up to hundreds of healthy mailboxes each day only to be brought up short by this one. While I know that "neither snow, nor rain, nor sleet, nor gloom of night stays these couriers from the swift completion of their appointed rounds," I wonder if this includes delivery to vertically challenged mailboxes.

Then again, maybe my neighbors don't mind being skipped. When's the last time you opened your mailbox without some vague sense of dread? Junk to sort, bills to pay, magazines depicting impossibly beautiful people you can become with one more diet, and who knows what else that will ruin your evening? Perhaps the fallen mailbox was passed by that first day and it came as a relief. No pile of accusing letters or flyers and catalogs to clutter up the counter. Peace! Maybe we should all get rid of our mailboxes. And while we're at it, cut the phone cords and the Internet connection and the cable, too. No news is great news! Joy!

Few in Bethlehem could have been as cut off from news as the shepherds on the hills. Who knows, they may have enjoyed their isolation. Peace! Joy! Yet, like some e-mail message that sneaks through your filter or a flyer stuck to your door, the heralds kept their appointed rounds. They got out of their mail truck, bent down, and slid the good news right into that mailbox anyway. "It's okay, guys, we know you are not too accustomed to good news. But that is what we're bringing you tonight!" Like the text message "luv u" that you don't mind getting, the thank-you note you never expected, or the headline that reads "Wall Street Rallies," this is news we can use. We might even tear down the firewalls around our hearts and the filters on our ears for news that a Savior—the embodiment of God's promise, the hope of the nations, the way out of this mess we are in—has come! Peace! Joy!

Maybe I should go out and help my neighbors repair that mailbox. Just think what good news they might be missing.

Questions to Ponder

- What is the best news you have ever received?
- What are some ways you could deliver the good news to someone who needs it today?

Prayer

God of peace and joy, send your messengers again today to bring us the good news of our Savior's birth. Break down the barriers of fear and apathy in our hearts, that we may join the shepherds in their headlong rush to the manger. Thank you for giving us the confidence that nothing can stop your joy from coming into our lives. Amen.

Day 16: Monday

Running into the Dawn

Psalm 30:1-12

Key Verse: For his anger is but for a moment; his favor is for a lifetime. Weeping may linger for the night, but joy comes with the morning. Psalm 30:5

I woke up early, my anemic watch alarm hardly necessary. I had been checking it hourly all night long. The first sleep away from home often goes that way for me. The travel, the new people and faces, and the broken routines both excite and unsettle my spirit. And there were other worries and fears in my heart not sloughed away by the miles driven or shucked off by the change in venue. Relieved to escape the stillness, where inner voices can be the loudest, I eagerly dressed for a long, purging run into the night.

I felt as much as saw my way through the darkness—not the beautiful pitch darkness that enrobes in velvet and is scattered with sequin stars. One can't run in such a blackout; one can only surrender and rest. But I plodded into the weary, washed-out night that was unhappily losing its battle with day. Beards of Spanish moss dangled, dead, parasitic, threatening. Vague shapes in fields stirred— my enemies lying in wait? Unseen ridges and ruts made my stride ungraceful. I'd like to say it was peaceful, but I was just not fleet enough to outrace my anxieties.

Turning around is the best moment in a long run. While it does not assure completion, it does grant relief, for now every costly step brings one closer to home. Not long down the return path, I thought I had lost my way. Surely on the way out I hadn't passed that charming farmhouse with the big red barn? Cows? Horses? Where had they come from? The road seemed smoother than I recalled, the air less brittle, the moss friendlier. But I was not lost. I was found. Found by the dawn, rising despite my worries and fears. Discovered there on the road, tear-stained from the night, laughing in the glow of it all. It was the same world I had wrestled with during that long night. But the sun exposed its beauty, its hope, and its promise. Joy in the morning. Somehow. Some way. God will bring joy in the morning. Run. Run. Run into the dawn.

Questions to Ponder

- Are you running from the darkness or into the dawn?
- How can we carry the joy of the dawn into the times in our lives when we must be in the twilight?

Prayer

Joy Giver, Dawn Bringer, open our eyes to see the day. Open our hearts to be filled with joy. Open our minds to know your promise. Open our spirits to know your hope. Be with us as we run into the dawn of this new day. We praise you for the joy that comes every morning. Amen.

Day 17: Tuesday

A Happy Ending

Proverbs 10:27-32

💬 *Key Verse:* The hope of the righteous ends in gladness, but the expectation of the wicked comes to nothing. Proverbs 10:28

My wife never wanted to see the movie *Titanic* because she knew how it was going to end—the boat sinks and lots of people drown. This criterion for selecting films to view certainly cuts back on our choices. But she has a good point. We both work in professions where we encounter people in difficult life situations. While they seek counsel and encouragement from us, we face the ever-present question: How is this all going to turn out for them? We don't know if they will find a way through their trials, and we may never know if they will find the peace and joy they seek. That is real life. So when it comes to "reel life," as in movie reels, it makes sense that my wife prefers movies that she knows will have a happy ending. Life has enough tragedy already.

Imagine now that you have been told that somehow, some way, the movie of your life is going to have a happy ending. You are given no reassurances that it will always be easy or comfortable or peaceful or happy. The only thing you are given is a promise that it will all turn out for good in the end. Would that knowledge make a difference to you when the rain comes? Would that information change the way you look at a failed business? Would that guarantee help you get up off the canvas for another round? Yes, I think it would. It would be a little secret that would keep the smile on your lips while others are sneering at you. It would be the rock to cling to when the tide rises. It would be the peace that you have that passes all understanding.

So hear it now: the hope of the righteous ends in gladness. Now, the righteous are not the perfect. The righteous are those who live by faith in the one who is perfectly good and totally in charge of how things turn out. This is the one who makes happy, joyful, holy endings of all sorts of beginnings and middles. In this movie, it is true that the storyline for most people of faith may not look much like a comedy. But look at the people closely. Their hearts are filled with joy, it is well with their souls, their eyes are on the prize, and their feet move with confidence. They know how it is going to end, because they know who writes the ending.

Questions to Ponder

- What examples of this truth have you read in Scripture and seen in your life?
- How does knowing that joy and gladness are waiting for us change your perspective on the tears and trials of each day?

Prayer

God of all beginnings and endings, reassure us today of our happy ending in you. Allow us to trust you so deeply that the tragedies of this world do not shake us, but rather send us to your arms. As you hold us and release us, remind us that all things end well that end in you. We pray this in the name of Jesus, the Alpha and Omega. Amen.

Day 18: Wednesday

Fast-Food Faith

Jeremiah 15:15-21

> *Key Verse:* Your words were found, and I ate them, and your words became to me a joy and the delight of my heart; for I am called by your name, O LORD, God of hosts. Jeremiah 15:16

Many children are going through the most important physical developments of their lives fueled by sugar-laced soda, chicken nuggets, and taco chips. On a recent TV show, a chef asked American schoolchildren to identify some raw vegetables as he held them up. They could not name many of the vegetables, including the potatoes and eggplants that he showed them. Perhaps their brains were a little sluggish, because some of the students had eaten pizza for breakfast in the cafeteria. Sure, they love those things, but the truth is they are not eating the kind of nutritious meals that will help them develop healthy minds and bodies.

Now for us adults the same might be said. The greater concern for us is that we stuff our souls with too much "junk food." The popularity of faux spirituality today has been both an indictment of the church's teaching ministry and a warning that hungry seekers will gobble up any attractive meal that is handy. Fast-food faith is full of empty calories that taste good for a moment: "Believe in yourself." "Make a miracle happen." "Follow your bliss." I recently heard a new song that was so full of spiritual clichés, I felt like I had eaten a dozen glazed doughnuts by the time it was over. We are wallowing in empty-calorie catch phrases and starving for something good to eat.

Jeremiah is in the midst of complaining about his prophetic ministry and the fate of his nation when he catches himself. He remembers that not too long ago, he ate God's words and found them healthy and nutritious. Good, there is hope for those of us who were fed carrots and beans and the Catechism and Bible stories to find our way back to good eats. There is no better meal than the one offered on any page of the Bible, and no tastier banquet than a Bible study at your own church. But what about those of us who can't recognize a psalm from a parable? Just as the chef is teaching children what is good for them, we must find new ways to reintroduce God's delicious commandments and satisfying promises to ourselves and our children. When we "taste and see," we will find that the Lord is good.

Questions to Ponder

- When was the last time you had a real meal of God's Word? How did it feed and strengthen you?
- What can you do to help your church serve up good meals for people hungry for more than fast-food faith?

Prayer

Giver of all good things, set before your people a feast that will bring them to the table and fill their aching bellies. Close our ears to empty advertisements for things that will not satisfy, and open our mouths to your good and gracious Word. Strengthen us by your Word and give us your joy. Amen.

Day 19: Thursday

Jesus Completes Us

John 15:7-11

> 💬 *Key Verse:* I have said these things to you so that my joy may be in you, and that your joy may be complete. John 15:11

In the film *Jerry McGuire* (Sony Pictures, 1996), Tom Cruise's self-centered character falls in love and utters these immortal words to his girl: "I love you. . . . You complete me." The vulnerability implied in that statement, that an ambitious, successful sports agent would be lacking in anything, makes it seem sweet and tender. But at base, it is still a self-centered statement. He loves her because she fills an empty space in his life. And here is the problem with romantic love. We think it is about them but it is always about us. When we need something different, they'd better be ready to fill that new space, or we may just have to find someone or something else to "complete us."

The truth is that even after marriage, couples are not complete. Selfishness doesn't magically disappear, and sin has a way of carving out new emptiness in each one of us. We cannot complete ourselves and we cannot complete anyone else. Jesus is the only one who can complete us. He wants to and he is able to. He who was without sin, yet gave himself up, has all the joy we could ever need to pour into us. The incompleteness inside us cries out, "I'm no good," and Jesus replies, "I have made you holy." The yawning gap between our intentions and our actions declares, "Judge me," to which Jesus shouts, "I take on your judgment and give you blessing instead." The million spaces of doubt between tiny pixels of faith threaten to engulf us in a black void. Then the baby and the blood and the cross and the empty tomb superimpose themselves on our blank screen and become our picture, our story, and our salvation.

Could there be a more tender and touching trio of chapters in all of Scripture than John 14, 15, and 16? After washing their feet and feeding them, Jesus speaks words of encouragement to the disciples: "Do not let your hearts be troubled" . "I will not leave you orphaned" (14:18). "Peace I leave with you" (14:27). called you friends" (15:15). "Your pain will turn into joy" (16:20). "Take courage; I have conquered the world!" (16:33). These words from Jesus complete the disciples, complete you, complete me, because Jesus gives not just words, but everything needed to back up those words and bring them to life. Though it will cost him everything we could never pay, it is his joy to make our joy complete.

Questions to Ponder

- Is your joy like Swiss cheese? What holes can you identify and pray for Jesus to fill?
- What would change if you looked to Jesus, and not to others, to complete you and make your joy complete?

Prayer

Dearest Savior, it is your joy to be our joy, your life to be our life, your hope to be our hope, and your peace to be our peace. Pour your blessings into our holey spirits and make them holy instead. Complete us and complete in us your will that brings joy to the world. Amen.

Day 20: Friday

Mixed Emotions

Matthew 28:1-10

💬 *Key Verse:* So they left the tomb quickly with fear and great joy, and ran to tell his disciples. Matthew 28:8

One year my son could not stop talking about the "Tower of Terror" ride at Disney's Hollywood Studios Theme Park in Orlando, Florida. (Actually, it's not much of a ride. It's more like being dropped 199 feet [60 m] in a broken elevator car.) He was just tall enough and brave enough to go on the ride that year. He did great on the way up, but when the elevator started to hurtle downward, he looked a little pale. When the ride stopped, I asked him if he was okay. He smiled victoriously, but when I asked him if he wanted to take the ride again, he didn't seem too eager. We stopped in the gift shop so he could rightfully don a well-earned T-shirt that said "I Survived the Tower of Terror." Fear mixed with joy—a potent mix for such a little guy.

Fear mixed with joy. This is what the women experience on that Sunday morning. Fear, still lingering in the air, as they trudge to Jesus' tomb. Joy, tinged with melancholy, to see him one more time. Fear again, as the earth shakes under their feet when they reach that hallowed ground. Fear, as the angel of the Lord descends. Joy, as the angel wrangles the stone away from the empty tomb. Joy at the news of the angel, "He's not here! You'll see him soon!" Joy, all joy, as Jesus greets them, as they touch him again. Joy, as they dash to share the good news with Jesus' fearful followers. Still a little fear, perhaps? After all, dead men are supposed to stay that way. Joy, then, mixed with fear. Happy Easter!

My son found fear and joy on a thrill ride. The women discovered fear and joy at Jesus' grave. Do we find fear and joy in our faith? Such a brew is too heady for many. Is it any wonder that we settle too often for a little less fear—even if that means a little less joy? We seek a faith of "happy mediums," where we never get too scared or take too many risks and are rewarded with a safe, comfortable salvation. We avert our gaze from the cross because it is a reminder that we are 'oin him there, each in our own way. As a result, the new life of faith is sort of like the old life, just a little nicer. But that's not why Jesus came and sneered at fear and died. He came to show us that to find his joy is worth facing all of our fears. Faith is a ride worth taking!

Questions to Ponder

- Think about a time when you let your fears steer you clear of true joy. What happened?
- What fears can you help others face so that they can know Jesus' joy?

Prayer

God of all joy, make us so obsessed with knowing the joy of your salvation that we boldly and bravely face all dangers and fears that come our way. May we, like the women at the tomb, come to know how Jesus' joy destroys our fear. Hear us from our depths and lift us to the heights of your joy. Amen.

Day 21: Saturday

Joys and Rejoicing

Philippians 4:4-7

> *Key Verse:* Rejoice in the Lord always; again I will say, Rejoice.
> Philippians 4:4

Three things about joy: joy starts small, joy grows, and joy is always a gift.

If you can learn to find joy in the small things, you can learn to find it anywhere. My mom finds joy in the colors of bird feathers ruffling in the breeze, tiny travelers who make a short layover in her backyard trees. My sister finds joy in the smell of yeast bubbling up from the beer she's brewing in her driveway on a chilly Sunday afternoon. I find joy when my calloused fingers touch chords on strings and wood sings familiar songs. These are little things, hardly worth mentioning and easily dismissed. A little like a baby, far from home, in a manger, so small. The world keeps looking for the next "big thing" and misses the tiny joy that starts so small.

Happiness is big and bombastic: "Look at me! Look at me!" But before you can turn, happiness has left the stage. Gut-wrenching guffaws and standing ovations accompany happiness, but too quickly they become echoes and memories. The lifespan of happiness is rarely equal to a human lifespan. Joy? Joy is the speck of sand in the oyster that becomes a pearl, the spindly sapling that fattens to an oak tree trunk, the first brushstroke on the blank canvas soon layered with color. Joy grows until it is more than happiness, more than sadness, more than disappointment, more than pain. So grows the toddler playing in his father's sawdust, the boy talking in the temple, the man walking out to the Jordan River. Pursue not happiness, but seek this joy.

A man snuffles as he rubs tears from his eyes. His grandchild's chubby hand reaches out to him with a refrigerator magnet that says "Mary Crismas." A husband laughs as he opens a gift box and sees the drill bits for the drill he sold to buy his love the charm for the bracelet she sold to buy him the bits. Sleepy big er is shocked to find the concert T-shirt he couldn't afford, given to him by his annoying little sister. She gasps as she opens his present to her, the last in the series of novels she's been secretly devouring.

Sometimes it is just like that. We get what we didn't know we wanted, and we get what we hardly realized we needed. Joys that could never be bought—only received. And the greatest joy, the joy from which all joy springs, the joy to the world and to the fishes in the deep blue sea, comes to you and to me. Do we need to be reminded again? Or does the small, but growing, gift of joy inside us propel us and compel us to rejoice and rejoice?

Questions to Ponder

- When has a small joy had a big impact on your life?
- How will you rejoice this Advent so that others may know of the greatest joy?

Prayer

Little baby, be our joy today. Come and inhabit the corners of our aching hearts and the wide expanse of our emptiness. Come and tickle our spirits that we may rejoice and rejoice and rejoice. Let our rejoicing lead others to the greatest joy! Amen.

Week 4: I Wonder about Peace

Day 22: Sunday

Where Is Peace?
1 Samuel 1:9-20

> *Key Verse:* Then Eli answered, "Go in peace; the God of Israel grant the petition you have made to him." 1 Samuel 1:17

He thought she was drunk. Her lips were moving, but he couldn't hear any words. He couldn't allow her to stay there, kneeling before the altar, mumbling and murmuring in her drunkenness.

His hands were shaking. He opened his mouth several times to speak, but the words simply wouldn't come. It was difficult to tell if he was going to burst into tears of desperation or break into screams of rage.

Her head was bowed so low that her chin nearly rested on her chest. She was breathing deeply, slowly, and releasing each breath forcefully. Asleep and snoring? Awake and sighing?

The first situation is Eli observing Hannah in the temple as she begged God to give her a child. The second, a man learning that his young daughter had died. The third, a friend searching for light within the darkness of clinical depression.

All of these faithful people were trying to make sense out of incomprehensible circumstances, looking for hope in the midst of nearly intolerable situations, and seeking ways to fill the gaping holes in their lives. Peace (the translation of the Hebrew word *shalom*) is not merely the absence of war. Peace is the presence of wholeness or completeness—the rest that comes from knowing that God is present in your life and is giving you all that you need to live a life of abundance. None of these three faithful people could claim such peace in the midst of their situations.

And yet Eli says to Hannah, "Go in peace," and promises, "The God of Israel grant the petition you have made to him." Hannah is blessed to bear a child, and she finds peace in giving life to her son. The grieving father has found something resembling peace. He no longer fears anything, not even death. "What is the worst that could happen? I could die?" he asks. "Then I'd see my little girl again. How could that be bad?" My friend would eventually find peace, through years of counseling and with the help of proper medications. She has now made her way to the end of that dark valley of despair.

Many of us struggle to find peace at some point in our lives. Perhaps we have not experienced situations as torturous as the three mentioned here, but we know what it is like to be unsettled and incomplete. The holidays may bring these feelings of discontent and brokenness even closer to the surface, as we set one less place at the table or worry about a clash between two guests who will be seated at that same table, or imagine the shattered life of one who may or may not show up for the family gathering. We might not anticipate as peaceful a gathering as the ones we see on Christmas cards. And yet we try to find hints of hope in the midst of our restless and broken lives.

Questions to Ponder

· When have you struggled to find peace?
· What reminds you of God's presence, even in the midst of those unsettling experiences?

Prayer

Prince of Peace, in the midst of unsettled and incomprehensible times, make us aware of your presence in our lives. Give us signs of your nearness and hints of hope. Bless us with shalom, so that we can begin to find healing and wholeness in the midst of our struggles. Amen.

Day 23: Monday

When Will Peace Come?

Isaiah 9:1-7

> *Key Verse:* For a child has been born for us, a son given to us; authority rests upon his shoulders; and he is named Wonderful Counselor, Mighty God, Everlasting Father, Prince of Peace. Isaiah 9:6

The dawn was beautiful. The horizon gradually changed colors—black, deep purple, shades of red, orange, yellow, hints of green, then the full blue of a new day. Beautiful . . . until one looked at the devastated landscape. What had been homes were piles of twisted rubble. Debris covered the once-pristine yards. What had been elegant trees were mangled and splintered twigs.

Whether destruction is caused by flood or hurricane, tornado or earthquake, or human disaster, such as war or explosion, the lives of the people involved are never the same again. What had been is gone, and with it all sense of stability and normality. Even a disaster that damages "only a part" of your home or your life, such as a fire or a robbery or an illness, brings the despair that comes with trying to fit all the pieces back together. No matter how many pieces are left, they never quite come together in the same way again.

Into the midst of this despair comes a promise: "The people who walked in darkness have seen a great light; those who lived in a land of deep darkness—on them light has shined" (Isaiah 9:2). The promised light is the birth of a child, and also the coming of a powerful ruler named "Wonderful Counselor, Mighty God, Everlasting Father, Prince of Peace." For those who have been walking in the valley of the shadow of death, dawn has come.

In Isaiah 9, it sounds as if the child is already among us, as if the coming of peace, healing, and wholeness is already complete. This was not the case for the people of Israel, however, who were still living in exile, whose homeland had been destroyed by war. It is not the case for people who wake up to the kind of destruction described above. It is not the case for many of us, as we try to hide our brokenness behind a smile, or struggle to see the beauty of the dawn in the midst of the debris of our lives.

Even as Isaiah describes the blessings that God has promised, his words are filled with images of war and warriors. The reality of his people's situation is not completely hidden behind the promise of better days to come. We too can name the pain and brokenness that have not yet been overcome, and at the same time describe a better day—one that we hope for, one that God has promised, one that we can imagine so vividly that it feels as if it could be here with us at any moment. The Prince of Peace will come, bringing the dawn of a new day.

Questions to Ponder

- What brokenness have you been hiding behind a smile or an "I'm fine" answer to the question, "How are you?"
- What is the promised future that you cling to and wait for God to bring to you?

Prayer

Wonderful Counselor, it is difficult to allow others to look into our brokenness. It is frightening to become vulnerable by sharing our pain. Help us to be honest with ourselves and with others, so that we can bear one another's burdens together and lighten our load by relying upon you. Amen.

Day 24: Tuesday

What Will Peace Look Like?

Zechariah 9:9-12

> 🗨 *Key Verse:* He will cut off the chariot from Ephraim and the war-horse from Jerusalem; and the battle bow shall be cut off, and he shall command peace to the nations; his dominion shall be from sea to sea, and from the River to the ends of the earth. Zechariah 9:10

"He said . . ." "She said . . ." "They started it!" When we fight, we engage in accusations, name-calling, or worse. A grudge can go so far back that no one remembers the original offense. And the nastiest of fights seem to happen within families, including church families. Instead of giving us a desire to make peace, knowing one another well only seems to provide quicker ways to drive the wounds in deep. No matter what the fights are about or who is involved in them, one truth comes forth again and again: there is a great shortage of peace in our world.

In the ancient world, peace came only when a ruler became powerful enough to snuff out all of the competition, when all were bloody and bruised and only one was left standing. Then when the end of a war was declared, peace meant oppression enforced by military might. Most people did not truly experience peace in such a world.

Zechariah envisions a new kind of peace. Peace brought by a powerful ruler, yes, but a ruler who does not ride into town on a warhorse followed by a parade of chariots and armed soldiers. This ruler rides a humble donkey, followed by the shouts and cheers of rejoicing people. This is true peace—*shalom*—the peace that brings wholeness and healing to all people. This peace is also bought with blood—the blood, sweat, and tears of one willing to be humble, to take a step down, to serve rather than demand to be served, to be sacrificed—the blood that Jesus shed upon the cross.

After the parade and shouts of joy, and before the sweat and tears in the Garden of Gethsemane and his bloody death on the cross, Jesus shared a quiet meal with his followers. In the midst of that meal, Jesus knelt and washed the feet of his disciples. It was a simple act of service, a recognition of a need waiting to be met, a gesture of kindness toward the people he loved. In the midst of the fighting, the demands, and the chaos that we call our daily lives, perhaps we also can share a simple act of service. Perhaps in that moment we can find the beginnings of peace and an opportunity to change the world.

Questions to Ponder

- Do you have any relationships that are teetering on the brink of destruction? How can a solid dose of humility on your part bring them back from the brink?
- In what ways can you follow the example of the King of kings in bringing peace into your home, your extended family, and your congregation?

Prayer

Mighty Lord, you have shown us what it means to be a gentle leader and a humble king. Help us to let go of our desire to be in control and to always have things our own way. Fill us with the peace that comes from knowing that our lives are resting safely in your hands. Amen.

Day 25: Wednesday

Who Will Bring Peace?

Luke 19:28-38

Key Verse: Blessed is the king who comes in the name of the Lord! Peace in heaven, and glory in the highest heaven! Luke 19:38

He was sitting in the recliner when the car pulled up. He was putting the footrest down when she walked into the room with her daughter cradled in her arms. As she leaned toward her father, she said to the baby, "Say hello to Grandpa." He was only 43 years old. It had not dawned on him, until that moment, that the birth of this child meant he was a grandfather. The moment of shock gave way to joy as the tiny girl was placed in his hands.

They threw their father a surprise 60th birthday party. One of the gifts was an eight-week-old black Lab puppy. Together the "kids" wrangled the puppy into a decorated box just before walking into Mom and Dad's house and calling, "Happy Birthday!" By the time the box was handed to the father, it was wiggling and squeaking. As the little black nose poked out of the box into his chest, surprise was transformed into a smile.

Situations such as these capture our attention. They are unexpected and filled with the joy of the moment. Nothing beyond that moment enters our minds. Nothing else matters. That instant is all that exists, and for that moment all is right with the world. The day that Jesus rode into Jerusalem on a donkey was a moment like this. Songs of praise and shouts of joy erupted spontaneously from the crowd that had gathered. A parade began to form. People who had been waiting for God to send them a Messiah were caught up in that moment of joyous excitement. Nothing else mattered, and all was right with the world. *Shalom*—the perfection of heaven and the glory of God's reign—was complete in that instant.

But it didn't last. Such moments never do. Within the week shouts of joy turned into cries of anger and hatred, the spontaneous parade of people became a mob bent on destruction, and the one who would be king was wearing a crown of thorns.

At this time of year, our thoughts are of a babe laid in a manger, not a lifeless body laid in a tomb. And yet these are both images of our king, who rode humbly into Jerusalem surrounded by the joyous cries of the people. The babe born in a stable would die on a cross. The one proclaimed king and Messiah would begin his reign by dying and rising again.

After Jesus' entry into Jerusalem, the next shouts of joy that we hear are those of Easter morning. "Alleluia! Christ is risen!" The one who can bring true peace—not for just a moment, but for all time—is the one who died and rose, never to die again.

Questions to Ponder

- What moments in your life have given you the feeling that all is right with the world? How do they connect with the joy and peace of Jesus' resurrection?
- How can you carry those moments and the power of Jesus' resurrection with you through other times when things are not so joy filled or peaceful?

Prayer

Everlasting God, you have promised that you will always be with us. You have also promised that we will spend eternity with you. Help us to bring moments of eternity into our daily lives, so that we can know the power of peace. Remind us that as dawn brings new light to the world, so you bring new life with each new day. Amen.

Day 26: Thursday

How Can We Prepare for Peace?

Luke 1:67-79

Key Verse: By the tender mercy of our God, the dawn from on high will break upon us, to give light to those who sit in darkness and in the shadow of death, to guide our feet into the way of peace. Luke 1:78-79

Shh . . . listen . . . what do you hear? The hum of the lights? The whoosh of warm air from the furnace? The ticking of the clock? The voices of your family? The bark of a dog? The slam of a car door? Silence? Have you ever heard silence?

Sometimes silence feels peaceful. When daily life is filled to overflowing with sounds and words and voices, we might welcome a few moments of "peace and quiet." When those daily sounds, words, and voices are harsh, silence also provides a retreat. And in silence we sometimes experience moments of connecting with God and listening for God's voice.

Sometimes silence is not so peaceful, however, as we rush to say something to fill a long pause in conversation, give the "silent treatment" to someone, or wait for the results of medical tests. Many of us turn on the TV or some music at any hour of the day or night, if only for "background noise." Silence can be uncomfortable too for people dealing with loneliness, illness, and other needs.

Imagine what it was like for Zechariah, who was silent for almost a year! He had offered the annual sacrifice and come out of the Holy of Holies unable to speak, and whatever had happened to him within the temple remained a mystery. Other than his lack of words, he was fine, so he and his family coped with his silence as well as they could. Using gestures and drawing in the dust of the ground were the only communication they had, until a week after his son was born.

As the community gathered to celebrate the circumcision of this miracle child, born late in the lives of Elizabeth and Zechariah, suddenly Zechariah found his voice restored. His first words came out as a song of praise, which we have received as the *Benedictus*—"Blessed be the Lord God of Israel." His hymn was not only a song of praise, but also a prophecy and a promise. John, the newborn child, would prepare the way for the Lord, speaking the promise of salvation and calling people to repentance for the forgiveness of their sins. And when the Messiah arrived, those who lived in darkness would see the light and be guided into the way of peace.

Shh . . . listen . . . listen for the silence.

Questions to Ponder

- What are the sounds and words that you generally hear in your daily life? Whose voices do you regularly hear? How do you experience silence?
- How will you use your voice today? Will others hear the voice of God in your words?

Prayer

Wonderful Counselor, you offer us words of hope and comfort, joy and peace. Help us to listen carefully to the voices around us. Bless us with voices to speak your words, so that we may bring the promise of peace to those around us and share your praises with our world. Amen.

Day 27: Friday

How Can I Help Others Find Peace?

Luke 2:8-20

> 💬 *Key Verse:* Glory to God in the highest heaven, and on earth peace among those whom he favors! Luke 2:14

As she entered the cafeteria, several classmates caught up to her and urgently asked, "What's the score?" They were coming from class. She was coming from the dorm. The Minnesota Twins were playing in the World Series. "I wasn't watching the game, but the Twins just scored and they either tied the game or went ahead," she replied. "How do you know what happened if you weren't watching the game?" she was asked. "Just before I left the dorm," she said, "the guys who live in the room above me started stomping on the floor and screaming."

In a popular YouTube video and song, a young boy asks, "Where is the line to see Jesus?" as he wanders in a shopping mall. There are plenty of other lines to wait in, including checkout lines and lines to see Santa. This child wonders why he can't find the line leading to the celebration of Jesus' birthday. "Where is the line to see Jesus?"

Perhaps the shepherds were asking that question, too. They probably thought that night would be peaceful and uneventful. They were not expecting an army of angels to invade the silence with an announcement of *shalom* for all of God's people. This sort of peace is something to be shouted from the housetops and celebrated with songs of praise! When an otherwise quiet night is interrupted by the appearance of angels singing praises to God, you might not know exactly what the score is, but you can bet that God is in the lead.

In our communities, Christmas celebrations seem to begin right after the Thanksgiving turkey has been turned into leftovers. Stores skip right from Halloween to Christmas, and so do the decorations in our neighborhoods. In the crowded malls and the busy streets, we may wonder if the commercialization of Christmas is winning, and where we can find the line to see Jesus.

Advent is a time set aside by the church to slow down and listen for God's quiet voice, to stop and let the shepherds come in from the fields. When the angels appear, then we will know what the score really is. We will know that God has won, and we will see Jesus, the good news of great joy that comes wrapped in bands of cloth and heralded with songs of praise. "Glory to God in the highest heaven, and on earth peace among those whom God favors!"

Questions to Ponder

- What lines do you spend the most time in these days? Where do you most often find yourself waiting? What are you waiting for?
- How can you help others join the line to see Jesus?

Prayer

Glorious God, fill us with your joy, so we can join with the angels in praising you. Fill us with your peace, so we can share it with others. Fill us with your good news, so we can point people to Jesus. Amen.

Day 28: Saturday

How Will I Recognize Peace When It Comes?

Luke 2:22-32

> 💬 *Key Verse:* Master, now you are dismissing your servant in peace, according to your word. Luke 2:29

How do I get from here to the ferry across the lake? "Go south on Washington—that's Main Street. Turn right onto Memorial Drive . . . you'll know it when you see it. You can't miss it." It was obvious when to turn onto Memorial Drive, because not turning would mean driving straight into Lake Michigan!

For Simeon, the appearance of the Christ child was just as obvious. Guided by the Holy Spirit, Simeon came to the temple. He walked up to Mary and Joseph, took the one-month-old baby Jesus into his own hands, and praised God. And in the midst of that praise, Simeon said that he was now ready to die, for he had seen the salvation of God with his own eyes.

How will we recognize the peace of God when it arrives in our own lives? Is it something that we "can't miss"? Will it be as obvious or shine as brightly as the Christmas trees and house decorations that have appeared in our neighborhoods? Or will it be hidden, a present that remains wrapped until we open it for ourselves? Consider this: How can you tell that milk is still good and has not turned sour? You recognize the smell. How can you tell that juice has not begun to ferment into vinegar or wine? You recognize the taste. Are there other smells and tastes that you recognize immediately? Cinnamon rolls? Easter lilies? A rose? Gingerbread? Your mother's perfume? These things are easy to recognize, because we live with them day after day after day, and they become familiar to us.

Simeon and the prophet Anna, who also met Jesus in the temple that day, show us a few ways to recognize the peace of God when it arrives—ways to become so familiar with God's presence that *shalom* will be something we cannot miss: prayer and devotion, worshiping God regularly, watching and waiting. When we fill our lives with the things of God—Scripture, worship, Christian community, prayer, and so on—we will see the power of God in our lives. We will recognize it because it is ingrained in us, because we know its familiar taste and smell, appearance and voice. It will be second nature, or perhaps first nature—the nature that comes from being baptized with the Spirit of God.

Simeon had seen God's *shalom*. Simeon had seen how God would bring all of the people of the world into peace, into a new relationship with God, a relationship that could never be broken. This child, this tiny baby, would bring people to God in a new way. He would bring redemption. He would bring forgiveness. He would bring new life. His coming would be the beginning of a new kingdom, the kingdom of heaven, the kingdom of God.

Questions to Ponder

- What are you doing to keep yourself immersed in God's Word and God's ways?
- In what ways are you watching and waiting for God's presence in your life?

Prayer

Wonderful Counselor, Mighty Lord, Prince of Peace, help us to hear your voice in the midst of this noisy season. Help us to see your face in the people whom we meet each day. Help us to be like Simeon and Anna—seeing your salvation and praising God for the wonders that have come into our lives through the birth of Mary's baby. Amen.

Bible Studies

Bible Study: Week 1

I Wonder about Hope

Psalm 146:5-7

Jeremiah 29:11

Romans 5:1-5

Romans 8:18-25

Ephesians 2:12-15

1 Thessalonians 4:13-14

1 Peter 1:3-7

In many congregations, the candle lit during the first week of Advent is called the Hope candle. How is hope connected to these four weeks before Christmas? Do we merely hope that we will make it through this often hectic time? The texts for this Bible study describe a hope that is not a wispy wish that things will turn out all right sometime in the future, but a bold, strong hope that is grounded in the death and resurrection of Jesus.

1. Discuss the following statement. Where does hope come from? Is it a choice?

> *Once you choose hope, anything's possible.*
> Christopher Reeve

_____

_____

_____

2. What hopes do you have for this Advent season? List as many things as you can, big and small.

_____

_____

3. Hope is discussed many times in Scripture. Brainstorm some reasons this might be the case. Why is hope difficult to come by and difficult to maintain?

_____

_____

4. Read the Bible texts listed above, and write down the truths about hope that you find. Which insight seems most helpful to you, and why? Draw or describe something that gives you hope.

_____

_____

5. Tell about someone you know who has a bold, strong hope grounded in the death and resurrection of Jesus.

_____

_____

6. Many people live in situations that seem hopeless. What are some ways you and your congregation can reach out to people who have lost hope?

_____

_____

7. What does hope have to do with Advent and the promise of the coming Savior? Why is Advent a time of hope?

_____

_____

Bible Study: Week 2

I Wonder about Love

> Luke 1:46-55
> Luke 4:16-30
> Luke 13:10-17

The candle lit during the second week of Advent is often called the Love candle. The Gospel of Luke shows us God's way of love and calls us to serve freely as part of God's love at work in the world.

1. Draw or describe what you think God's love is like.

_____

_____

2. Have volunteers read aloud the three Bible texts listed above. Using pencil and paper, as each text is read draw a horizontal line that goes up when the lowly are lifted up and goes down when the lofty are brought low. What do you see?

_____

_____

3. Martin Luther used his "theology of the cross" to describe how God works in the world. He said God often works through the unexpected, unlikely, and lowly. How is God at work in this way in Mary's song in Luke 1:46-55?

_____

_____

4. Early in Jesus' ministry, he visited his hometown of Nazareth, read from Isaiah 61:1-2 in the synagogue, and then proclaimed that this Scripture was being fulfilled (Luke 4:16-30). The people were amazed, but later they tried to run Jesus out of town. What do you think of the people's reaction? If you had been there in the synagogue, how would you have reacted?

_____

_____

_____

5. Have four volunteers act out the story as Luke 13:10-17 is read again. The volunteers play the parts of the bent-over woman, the synagogue leader, the crowd, and Jesus. Change parts and act out the story again. How does being low ("bent over") or being high (in a position of authority) affect what you see and hear? What character in the story is most like you, and why?

_____

_____

_____

6. Where do you see God's love at work in the world today? How are you and your congregation part of this work?

_____

_____

Bible Study: Week 3

I Wonder about Joy

Genesis 21:1-7

Isaiah 12:1-6

Isaiah 51:1-11

Isaiah 55:6-13

The candle lit during the third week of Advent is often called the Joy candle. What is joy? Is it just another word for happiness? Throughout Scripture, God gives joy, even in the most desperate and hopeless situations. Does God give us joy yet today?

1. What words, phrases, images, and songs come to mind when you think about joy? List things that bring you joy.

_____

_____

_____

2. Abraham and Sarah lived in ancient times and were long past their child-bearing years when God promised them a son and many descendants. Read Genesis 21:1-7, the story of the birth of their son. What did Isaac's birth mean to Abraham and Sarah? How did that birth bring joy?

_____

_____

_____

3. The people of Israel had been captured and forced into exile in Babylon. The words of Isaiah 55:6-13 promised that God would lead the people out of Babylon and back to their homeland. What do you think this return would mean to the people who had lived in exile? How might it bring joy?

_____

_____

4. The people of Israel waited for centuries for a Messiah or Savior to come. After Jesus was born, angels announced the good news to shepherds taking care of their flocks of sheep. Read about this in Luke 2:8-20. What did Jesus' birth mean to the shepherds? How did that birth bring joy to them?

_____

_____

5. What do you think about the following statement?

   Happiness comes and goes. Joy grows until it is more than happiness, more than sadness, more than disappointment, more than pain.

_____

_____

6. What does Jesus' birth mean to us? How does that birth bring us joy? What blessings of God do you feel like singing about today? Look through a hymnal or songbook. This Advent season, what song of joy would you choose to sing to God?

_____

_____

Bible Study: Week 4

I Wonder about Peace

John 14:15-31

Philippians 4:4-9

The candle lit during the fourth week of Advent is often called the Peace candle. We have been wondering and wandering through God's word for three weeks now, and Christmas is drawing near. This week our lives will reach the climax of the chaos that we call "the holiday season." Into this self-imposed craziness comes one who would be known as Prince of Peace. And so we wonder and wander a little longer, as we imagine the peace that our Lord can bring to our lives.

1. Begin by reading John 14:15-31. In this passage, Jesus is saying good-bye to his followers in the gentlest way possible. He knows that in the next few days he will suffer and die, and yet he speaks to them of peace. Make a list of Jesus' final instructions. How do these instructions help his followers prepare for what is to come? How does Jesus' promise of peace fit within these final instructions?

_____

_____

2. Look over the *list* of instructions from question 1. What insights do these instructions give you for dealing with situations in the next week and your Christmas activities? How do they prepare you for life beyond the holiday?

_____

_____

3. Read Philippians 4:4-9. Although the apostle Paul was not writing to the people in Philippi about Christmas celebrations or gatherings, his words seem to speak directly to our busyness during the Holy Season. List several things that make you anxious or are creating anxiety for you this week. Make another list of things, people, and events that you are thankful for—even if they are making your life less peaceful right now.

_____

_____

4. Name one thing you can do that will help you focus on the joy and thankfulness of Christmas, rather than the busyness and anxiety. Then name one thing you can choose *not* to do, so that you can focus on the joy and thankfulness of Christmas.

_____

_____

5. Write a prayer in which you present all these things—your anxieties, your joys, your relationships, and whatever else comes to mind—to God. Ask for God's help in these matters and in showing gentleness in all you do.

_____

_____

_____

6. Close by reading aloud together this blessing based on Numbers 6:24-26.

The Lord bless you and keep you,
The Lord's face shine on you with grace and mercy.
The Lord look upon you with favor and give you peace.
Amen. (*ELW*, p. 14)

Activities

Week 1: I Wonder about Hope

Wonderful Luminaries: Hope Shines in the Darkness
Watch this activity build during the Advent season.

Materials needed: four empty tin cans (all the same size, such as coffee cans; or four different sizes, perhaps in descending order of size from large to small); spray paint (optional); water and a freezer; permanent black marker or paper, printer, and tape; a hammer and nails or an electric drill and drill bits; four battery-operated candles

Time required: 30 minutes (not counting the time it takes for the water to freeze in the cans overnight)

afety precautions: An adult should handle opening and cleaning the cans, ay painting (optional), and hammering or drilling holes in the cans. Turn on battery-operated candles and carefully drop them into the cans, rather than putting your hand inside the cans.

1. Talk about Advent and the four-week "wondering" you will be doing together as a family.

2. Remove and recycle the top lids from the cans. Make sure the cans are clean and dry and that any inside edges are smooth. If you wish, an adult can spray paint the cans in your choice of color.

3. Use the black marker to print the words *Hope, Love, Joy,* and *Peace* on the front of each can, one word per can. Create each letter with evenly spaced dots rather than straight lines. Another option is to choose a font on your computer and print out the words to use as a pattern. If you decide to do this, you can tape the paper on the can after it has been in the freezer.

4. Fill the cans with water and put them in the freezer overnight.

5. Once the water has frozen, remove the Hope can from the freezer. Use the hammer and nails or drill and drill bits to poke through the dots on the can or follow your pattern to make dots, spelling out *Hope.* The ice in the can creates a firm surface to hammer or drill through.

6. Set the can in warm water to dislodge the ice. Remove and dry the can.

7. Either now or in the coming weeks, repeat steps 5 and 6 to prepare the Love, Joy, and Peace luminaries.

8. Turn on a battery-powered candle and set it in the Hope luminary. Set the Hope luminary outside on your steps, porch, or deck or along a walkway. Gather together and watch the way the candle lights up the word *Hope.*

9. Light the luminary each evening during the first week of Advent. Discuss the ways that you find hope in everyday events, conversations, and tasks. Wonder together about the theme of hope, and pray about any concerns or reasons for thankfulness you may have.

Mini Advent Wreath

Make a personalized desktop Advent wreath!

Materials needed: a circular wooden curtain ring and four birthday candles for each person; electric drill and drill bit; an assortment of small Christmas decorations or ornaments; artificial greenery; ribbon or metallic chenille stems; glue

Time required: 20 minutes, not counting preparation

Safety precautions: An adult should do the drilling ahead of time. Do not leave lit candles unsupervised.

1. Drill four holes in each of the rings, large enough for a birthday candle to fit snugly in each hole.

2. Without covering up the holes, wrap rings with ribbon or metallic chenille stems, then glue on pieces of greenery, ribbon, and small Christmas ornaments or decorations.

3. Insert one birthday candle into each hole in the rings.

4. As you are working on your mini Advent wreaths, tell your family that people in many homes and churches celebrate this season by lighting one candle in an Advent wreath the first week, two candles the second week, three the third week, and four the fourth week. Christmas comes during the fourth week each year.

Sweet Scents Pinecones

Let my prayer be counted as incense before you, and the lifting up of my hands as an evening sacrifice. Psalm 141:2

Let the scents of the season surround you with these festive pinecones, or make a sweet-smelling gift for someone special.

Materials needed: an assortment of large pine cones; white glue; ground cinnamon; glitter; a can or jar with a lid; a shaker-top can or jar (such as a cheese shaker); newspaper; a plain empty box; a festive basket or box; twine, raffia, or ribbon

Time required: 10 minutes, not counting time to find the cones or drying time

1. Collect an assortment of pine and fir cones. Have everyone help with this, if possible.

2. Pour the ground cinnamon and glitter in the can or jar, cover with the lid, and shake to mix. Transfer the cinnamon-glitter mix to the shaker.

3. Line the bottom of the plain box with several layers of newspaper.

4. Working with one cone at a time, drop white glue randomly on each cone. You might make polka-dots with the glue, draw a line of glue along the edge of the cone petals, or come up with your own ideas.

5. Shake, shake, shake! Working over the box, shake the cinnamon-glitter mix onto the glue liberally, then turn the cones over and shake any excess into the box.

6. Set the cones aside to dry, then put them in a festive box or basket and tie a ribbon around it.

Wondering about Symbols Treasure Hunt

What will we see when we really look?

Materials needed: paper, pencils or markers, digital camera (optional)

Time required: daily walk or drive time

1. Talk together about symbols of the season as well as symbols of the Christian faith, such as a Christmas tree, a star, a manger, a crown, holly, a wreath, a candle and its flame, a cross, Christmas lights, and a lamb. (Consult a book or other resource if you would like to add to this list.)

2. Make a list of the symbols you would like to search for by drawing or writing them on paper.

3. When you take a walk or daily drive to work, school, or childcare, look for items on your list. How many times do you see each symbol? Keep track of what you see and share the results at the end of each day.

4. You might want to make a chart to keep a tally for the entire season of Advent. Post it on your refrigerator or bulletin board or in another central place in your home.

Optional: Use a digital camera to take a photo of each symbol you see. Print the photos as a visual reminder of your treasure hunt.

Button Pendant Ornaments

Button, button, who's got the button?

Materials needed: chenille stems, assorted colorful buttons (each with two or four holes), ribbon or raffia, scissors

Time required: 10–15 minutes

Safety precautions: Use this activity with kids who are five or older. (The buttons could present a choking hazard for very young children.)

1. Collect an assortment of buttons of different colors and sizes.

2. Have fun sorting the buttons by different characteristics. For example, sort the buttons by those with two holes or those with four holes. Put all the red buttons together, all the blue buttons together, and so on. Make a pile of round buttons and a pile of square buttons. What are some of the other ways you can sort the buttons?

3. Now take a chenille stem and bend it into a U shape. Put each button through one of its holes onto the chenille stem and slide it down, making a stack of buttons on one side of the "U." Leave a few inches of the chenille stem empty on top of the stack of buttons.

4. Bend the empty side of the chenille stem through one of the holes in the bottom button. Keep threading the chenille stem through the rest of the buttons, from the bottom to the top.

5. Twist the ends of the chenille stem together to make a loop to hang the ornament from a Christmas tree or in a window as a decoration.

Optional: It would be fun to make patterns with the buttons, such as red-green-red-green or other color combinations, to add a little more interest to the creation process!

Week 2: I Wonder about Love

Wonderful Luminaries: Love Shines in the Darkness

Let hope and love shine for all to see.

Materials needed: Hope luminary from last week, Love luminary, battery-operated candles

Time required: 30 minutes (not counting freezing the water in the can overnight)

1. If you did not prepare the Love luminary last week, look back at pages 80–81 for the instructions on how to make it for this week. Make sure the water is frozen when you are ready to begin hammering or drilling.

2. Talk about how the first week in Advent went and what signs of hope you may have seen, heard, or experienced in your daily life together.

3. If necessary, turn on a battery-powered candle and put it in the Hope luminary.

4. Set the Love luminary outside next to the Hope luminary, and insert the battery-powered candle. Gather together and watch the way the candle lights up the word *Love.*

5. Turn on the candles each evening during the second week of Advent. Discuss the ways that you share love in everyday events, conversations, and tasks, and the special times of love this season brings. Hold hands and pray together, thanking God for the love you have as a family and in God's family.

Heart-Shaped Tasty Treats

Celebrate the love in your family and in God's family.

Materials needed: a favorite family recipe for brownies, crispy rice cereal treats, pancakes, or even toast; recipe ingredients; baking supplies; mixing bowls, pans, and utensils; heart-shaped cookie cutters, molds, or baking pans; red berry jam (optional)

Time required: mixing and baking time for your favorite recipe, about 30-45 minutes

Safety precautions: Let young children help as much as possible, but an adult should be responsible for the use of the stove, oven, griddle, or toaster.

1. If you will need to use an oven, check the recipe for preheating instructions and temperatures.

2. Follow the recipe and baking instructions to make heart-shaped treats to share.

3. If you make brownies or crispy rice cereal treats, let them cool in the pan, then turn the cookie cutter in an alternate pattern to cut as many heart-shaped treats as you can. If you are making pancakes, put a heart-shaped mold onto the frying surface and pour the pancake dough into it. Let set and then remove the mold to make another pancake. If you are making toast, remove toast from the toaster and press a heart-shaped cookie cutter into it to cut out a heart. Be sure to add red berry jam to the toast before you take a bite!

Stained Glass Hearts

Love lets the light shine through!

Materials needed: waxed paper, old crayons, a cheese grater or vegetable peeler, newspaper, heart-shaped cookie cutters, iron, ironing board, scissors, hole punch, ribbon or yarn

Time required: 15–20 minutes

Safety precautions: Use the cheese grater or vegetable peeler carefully to prevent cuts. An adult should handle the iron and not leave it unattended.

1. Place several layers of newspaper on the ironing board and cover with a large sheet of waxed paper.

2. Set the iron on low or warm.

3. Using the cheese grater or vegetable peeler, grate a variety of shades of old crayons into a pile on the waxed paper. Using a range of shades, such as light pink to dark pink to red to purple, will make an interesting design.

4. Once you have a good pile of crayon shavings, spread them around on the waxed paper to cover almost all of it. Leave about 2 inches (5 cm) along the edges of the paper clear.

5. Tear off another sheet of waxed paper and lay it over the crayons. Spread several thicknesses of newspaper on top.

6. Gently but firmly begin pressing the newspaper, using a slow circular motion so that you cover the entire waxed paper area. As the crayons begin to melt, you will smell the wax and also see it begin to seep into the newspaper.

7. To check to see if the crayons have melted, lift up one corner of the newspaper and peek under it. The time to melt all of the wax and fuse the two pieces of waxed paper together will vary, depending on the thickness of the crayon shavings.

8. Once the waxed paper is melted, remove the newspaper and see how the waxed paper is fused together. After it cools completely, cut heart shapes from the waxed paper or trace around several cookie cutters and cut the hearts out.

9. Punch holes in the top of the hearts and tie pieces of ribbon or yarn through the holes for hanging on a Christmas tree, on gift packages, or in a window where the light will shine through the hearts like stained glass!

Wreath of Names

I have called you by name, you are mine. Isaiah 43:1b

Keep the names of people you know and love close to your heart during Advent.

Materials needed: white poster board, green markers, wide red ribbon, scissors, glue or stapler

Time required: 20 minutes

1. Cut the poster board into a large circular wreath shape.

2. Cut and tie the red ribbon into a large bow and glue or staple it to the wreath at the bottom edge.

3. Hang the wreath in a central place in your home, such as on a kitchen cupboard or a hallway closet door.

4. As you receive Christmas cards, letters, or greetings throughout the season of Advent, use a green marker to write the names of the senders on the wreath. You might choose to write the names in a circular format around the wreath, or you might print them radiating from the center out to the edge.

5. Try to fill the entire wreath with the names of family members and friends. Use the wreath as a meeting place for a time of family prayer or devotions to begin each day, or just before bedtime each night.

Week 3: I Wonder about Joy

Wonderful Luminaries: Joy Shines in the Darkness

Joy lights up our lives!

Materials needed: Hope and Love luminaries from last week, Joy luminary, battery-operated candles

Time required: 30 minutes (not counting freezing the water in the can overnight)

1. If you have not prepared the Joy luminary, look back at pages 80–81 for the instructions on how to make it for this week. Make sure the water is frozen when you are ready to begin hammering or drilling.

2. Talk about how the second week in Advent went, and what signs of love you may have seen, heard, or experienced in your daily life together.

3. If necessary, turn on the battery-powered candles and insert them in the Hope and Love luminaries.

4. Set the Joy luminary outside, next to the Hope and Love luminaries. Turn on a battery-powered candle and insert it in the Joy luminary. Gather together and watch the way the candle lights up the word *Joy*.

5. Turn on the candles each evening during the third week of Advent. Discuss the ways that you find joy in everyday events, conversations, and tasks, and the special times of joy this season brings. Hold hands and pray together, asking God to show you how to share the joy of your faith with others this week.

Sweet Stirrers

Mmmm . . . sweet treats to share!

Materials needed: 5-inch (13 cm) peppermint sticks, white melting chocolate, wooden spoon, glass mixing bowl, baking sheet, parchment paper, white or red sprinkles

Time required: 10–15 minutes

Safety precautions: The bowl used for melting may be hot when it is removed from the microwave.

1. Line a baking sheet with parchment paper.

2. Follow the instructions on the white chocolate for melting it using a microwave oven and a glass bowl.

3. Once the chocolate is melted, dip one end of each peppermint stick into the bowl of chocolate, covering about half of the stick with chocolate.

4. Place the peppermint sticks on the baking sheet, letting the chocolate set slightly for about 5 minutes.

5. Roll the chocolate ends of the sticks in the white or red sprinkles and return to the baking sheet.

6. Let stand at room temperature until the chocolate has hardened.

7. Eat as is or stir into hot cocoa or a favorite coffee drink.

Starry Night Candleholders

Stars are part of the wonderful world God created.

Materials needed: clear glass votive candleholders; shiny gold and silver star stickers; gold and silver pens that can write on glass surfaces; wax or battery-operated votive candles or tea lights

Time required: 10 minutes

Safety precautions: Do not leave burning candles unattended.

1. Purchase clear glass votive candleholders and silver and gold star stickers.

2. In the evening, talk about some of the wonderful things God created, including stars in the sky. Then go outside or look out a window. If the stars are out, can you count them?

3. Place star stickers on the candleholders in a variety of patterns or designs: all gold or silver, a combination of gold and silver, in a random pattern, or in rows around the entire candleholder

4. Use the pens to add stars, squiggles, swirls, or other designs to the glass.

5. Put a candle in the candleholder and enjoy the light of the stars shining through the glass!

Good News Prayers

Do you wonder sometimes if there is any good news in the world? Jesus is good news!

Materials needed: daily newsprint newspapers or online newspapers, chart paper, markers, tape

Time required: 10 minutes daily

1. Cut a piece of chart paper to fit on your refrigerator or bulletin board or somewhere else in a central place in your home.

2. Label the chart "Good News Prayers" and talk together about using the daily newspapers as a source of conversation and prayer.

3. Plan a time to meet near the "Good News Prayers" chart with a newspaper and marker on a regular basis.

4. At your scheduled time, look over the news, either individually or together, and talk about what is going on in the world. Talk about the good news and the bad news—and make note of people, events, and places in the world in need of prayer during this time of Advent. Write these prayer concerns, names, and other references on the chart.

5. Pray that all of these people and places will experience the joy of knowing Jesus. Be sure to date the prayers, and add a date when you see an answer to a prayer concern.

6. As you and your family receive Christmas cards during the season of Advent, you may want to add the names of friends and family members to the "Good News Prayers" as well.

Holiday Lights Wreath

The people who walked in darkness have seen a great light. Isaiah 9:2

Light up your home and neighborhood with the joyful light of the Advent season.

Materials needed: recycled wire wreath forms, white or colored Christmas lights, extension cord

Time required: 10–15 minutes

1. Purchase or repurpose several strings of outdoor white or colored Christmas lights.

2. Wrap the strings around the recycled wire wreath form multiple times, covering the wreath as completely as possible.

3. Hang the wreath outside your home. Attach an extension cord and plug it into an electrical outlet.

Week 4: I Wonder about Peace

Wonderful Luminaries: Peace Shines in the Darkness
Let all four of your Advent lights shine!

Materials needed: Hope, Love, and Joy luminaries from the previous weeks;
Peace luminary; battery-operated candles

Time required: 30 minutes (not counting freezing the water in the can
overnight)

1. If you have not prepared the Peace luminary, look back at pages 80–81 for the
   instructions on how to make it for this week. Make sure the water is frozen
   when you are ready to begin hammering or drilling.

2. Talk about how the third week in Advent went and what signs of joy you may have seen, heard, or experienced in your daily life together.

3. If necessary, put fresh batteries in the candles. Turn them on and insert them in the Hope, Love, and Joy luminaries.

4. Set the Peace luminary outside next to the Hope, Love, and Joy luminaries. Turn on a candle and insert it. Gather together and watch the way the candle lights up the word *Peace*.

5. Turn on the candles each evening during the fourth week of Advent. Talk about the peace we feel this time of year, the peace that we long for personally, and the peace we long for throughout the world. Hold hands and pray together, thanking God for peace in the world.

P-E-A-C-E Game Cards

How do you spell *PEACE?*

Materials needed: old BINGO cards or cardstock and a marker to make your own cards, red or green buttons to use as game markers, alphabet game pieces to use for calling the letters

Time required: 5 minutes to make the cards; time will vary for playing the game

1. Change the letters on BINGO cards to spell PEACE. If you do not have old BINGO cards, make your own cards using cardstock and markers.

2. Add numbers to the alphabet game pieces to correspond with the PEACE cards.

3. Decide who will be the person calling the letters and numbers, and distribute all game cards and buttons.

4. Play the game. The first person to get "PEACE" (a complete horizontal, vertical, or diagonal row) wins that round.

5. Try different variations of BINGO games, such as three-in-a-row, diagonal rows only, blackout, and others you may know.

Tile Coasters

Keep these tile coasters on your desk or coffee table as a daily reminder of God's gift of peace.

Materials needed: small white ceramic tiles (such as bathroom or kitchen tiles), ceramic paint or vinyl "clings," brushes, water, towels, newspaper

Time required: 10 minutes, not including paint-drying time

1. Cover a table with newspaper if you are using paint.

2. Talk or think about signs and symbols for peace, such as a dove, an olive branch, or a peace symbol.

3. Use the ceramic paint to paint your own peace symbols on the tiles. Let them dry according to paint instructions. You could also use vinyl "clings" to decorate your tiles.

4. You might prefer to make one tile with each of the words used during the four weeks in *Advent Reflections*: Hope, Love, Joy, and Peace.

5. Cold or hot drinks can be set on your completed tile coasters.

Yummy Cookie Mixes

Sharing with others increases the joy and peace in which we live as children of God.

Materials needed: one 1-quart (1 l) widemouthed jar and lid for each cookie mix; wooden spoon, measuring cups, and measuring spoons; baking ingredients; fabric, ribbon, small ornaments, or other embellishments for the jar lid; index cards; hole punch

Time required: 10 minutes

1. Choose a favorite cookie mix recipe or use the oatmeal cookie mix recipe on page 96.

2. Follow directions in each recipe for layering the dry cookie mix ingredients in the wide-mouth jar. After layering, seal with the lid.

3. Write the recipe instructions on an index card, or photocopy the recipe below. Punch a hole in the recipe card and tie a ribbon through it, attaching it to the jar lid. Add other embellishments to the jar lid, such as a circle cut from fabric and fastened to the lid with ribbon, raffia, or twine. Tie small ornaments or decorations to the ribbon as an added touch.

4. Make several yummy cookie mixes to share with a local food bank or families in need.

Oatmeal Cookie Mix

1⅓ cups (320 ml) quick-cooking oats
½ cup (120 ml) packed brown sugar
½ cup (120 ml) white sugar
½ cup (120 ml) chopped nuts
1 cup (240 ml) chocolate chips
1 cup (240 ml) flour
1 tsp. (5 ml) baking powder
1 tsp. (5 ml) baking soda
½ tsp. (2.5ml) salt

Layer the first five ingredients in the jar, packing each ingredient layer firmly before adding the next ingredient. Combine the remaining ingredients in a small bowl and mix well. Layer this mixture in the jar and secure the lid.

Baking instructions:
Mix cookie ingredients in a large bowl. Add ½ cup (120 ml) melted butter, 1 beaten egg, and 1 tsp. (5 ml) vanilla extract. Mix well. Shape dough into 1-inch (2.5 cm) balls and arrange on a lightly greased baking sheet. Bake at 350ºF (180ºC) for 11 to 15 minutes, then cool for 5 minutes before moving to wire cooling racks. Makes 2-1/2 dozen cookies. Yum!